The Book of John

A collection of Poem, Prose, and Rhyme by

Marcus C. John

To Jessica

Thank you

for supporting

Please Enjoy

Peace

Marcus C. John

DEDICATION

To every Spirit from birth to present moment
thank you

CONTENTS

Part 1

1:27 Do You? Haiku #1

2:27 Respiration

3:27 Heavy the Head

4:27 Sunshine over the Water

5:27 Road Work Haiku #2

6:27 Dear

7:27 Blunt Speech

8:27 Miseducation of the Brown

9:27 Punctuation

Part 2

10:27 Open the Door Haiku #3

11:27 The Lover

12:27 Teal Tercet

13:27 Mama's Boy

14:27 I Can See in Color

15:27 SNAP

16:27 Wakanda haiku Haiku #4

17:27 Ballad Mongers

18:27 The Acrobat

Marcus C. John

Part 3

19:27 Release Me Haiku #5

20:27 The RelationShip

21:27 Sound Doctrine

22:27 Get Me Bodied

23:27 Holy Crap! Haiku #6

24:27 Symbols

25:27 SpirituaList

26:27 Worry Free

27:27 ...In Conclusion

ACKNOWLEDGEMENTS

Special thanks to
Editors Kumi Owusu and Ibrahim Siddiq
Photographer Julie Cousens
Cover Designer Tyreek Kidd
and all extensions of my Family for support

The Book of John

Part 1

/

<u>Do you?</u>
Haiku #1

I've mastered getting up
by remembering the reason
for the fall…

<u>Respiration</u>

May the dirt brushed off your shoulders

become the soil you plant your seed of recovery in

Then grow

into yourself

inhalation is essential

your image remains valid

the experience will be an asset

change is a good thing.

We, the directors

never meant to fall in love with the story

simply read the script

produce with purpose,

then project for all to see.

This life is post production

you've been narrating the whole time

is this poem in your voice or mine?

Sometimes we believe we've been separated from the divine

stuck living a life that always feels odd,

in what scene did you forget that you were God?

Breathe.

Remember…

Marcus C. John

<u>Heavy the Head</u>

Ready, always spinning…
we crouch low, burrowed into homes, spaces known and familiar
I AM, the first and the last piece
The Alpha, The Warrior, The Mother
I shake and break the ground
a red clay woman
plunging into rising waters,
deep into rivers of sensuality
Intuition explored. Splashing into awareness,
sexuality matures.
I FEEL as though I have been here before.
A clementine wave, resembling a ripple in time, warns me to
think before I speak to moons and watch out for
Fire!! I need to be cautious with what I DO with this. Attention
feeds the flame, I don't mirror the mirrors, I break through
remembering the warmth of the Sun, while being addled by the sparks,
not succumbing to the dark, building bridges to the heart
a yellow belly connecting to a proud chest
opening up to shoulders with wings attached
Freedom felt in flight as harmony leads the way
My old reflection for I LOVE you but I can not stay
A chariot awaits in the distance, driven by internal desires
I rise on the side of dragons, facing heaven and greener pastures
Compelled to fill my lungs with cleaner qualities of Air
beyond smog, fog, and despair.
I evaporate, filter and cohabitate, audible;
humanity has a hero they can see and hear
Protect the neck, be still, be paced, be honest
I SPEAK in truth, with love, with Power
responsible with response,
Leadership in the literature, melodies for the melodrama
spells and hymns to cure the Blues
spiral up the scale,

see the keys?
see the key?
I SEE. arpeggio across the mind
unlocking each indentured thought, redefined
Free from confinement or
the refinement of ideas, ideals, we deal with the blind.
Two eyes is only half of what we see with the third
The middle of the mental balancing polarities of space and time,
royal, sharp, clear and decalcified,
Eye UNDERSTAND and Overstand.
Compassion in cloud form:
rain can dampen a day or lend life to lavender
The ability to envision and experience existence abstract
and as all parts,
participating in all roles
pro and antagonist, creator and destroyer,
teacher and student, parent and child,
The Omega. The Guru, Baba,
The Crown. You are divine!
Heavy the head but strongest the will.
All embraced and in alignment.
We wear our virtues in bold color,
omnipotent, and reflective to light;
casting away shadows as we saunter with regality and pride.
Linear by design, life has a stride but my kind prefer spirals

Marcus C. John

<u>Sunshine Over the Water</u>

Sunshine over the water casts a familiar feeling in the air
the belief in the fact that a new day is upon us
light bestowed onto the awoken, eyes open toward the present
gifted voices chirp to speak manifesting what they sing
today is the day for everything. tomorrow a hope and a prayer
yesterday was never here

Sunshine over the water welcomes the wind with open arms
accepting change as it blows like a trumpet over the scene
trees become piano keys and play a rhythm as they're stroked
the breeze directs the waves to perform percussion on the beat
your hips won't deceive, they'll come alive when they hear it
toes tap to the lyrics, all while the hook sounds so sweet

Sunshine over the water ignites the fires to burn for clarity
the blind now able to witness truth
the living dead who hunt for warmth find solace in the heat
those who roam this land in search of home
find a place where they can remember destinies
the directions are in the reflection
when was the last time you took a peek?

Sunshine over the water connects the Heavens and the Earth
lessening the distance between us and our origin
soul selves in full view, still connected to the ground
becoming the star, the pebble, and all that exists in the middle
it makes you wonder how those granted with so much
can be thankful for so little

<u>Road Work</u>
Haiku #2

Ego drives society;
must focus where
I park my attention

Marcus C. John

<u>Dear</u>

I wanted to write you·a formal letter
but always had trouble scribing
formal letters begin with dear, and
by putting that before your name
I knew I would be lying

A book describes our tale more accurately
with a preadolescent prologue, I was
amazed by your front cover and iridescent design
followed every direction on your literary trail
then held onto your sentences like brail
my love was blind. Eyes too green
to see between the lines that were drawn
knew you were the author of previous muses scorned
but I was the main character in this story

Stormy the conditions of our setting
your mood choppy like the sea when it rages
hoping this ship would sail as smooth as paper
instead I'd watch the tide turn like pages.
Searching for a true definition, usually settling for the synonym,
we called it home. What would seem like change,
always remained the same, you were a palindrome
I had it backward

Saw this dog as a God who tried to fetch my holy spirit
dug a ditch inside my heart so deep nobody could repair it
I was given all the tools but didn't know how to use them
received attention and abuse but confused them
you used affection as a noose
the truth was gruesome

Hung onto the idea that I could keep reading into
this chapter of my life that no longer defined me

John 1

finally penned the appendix of our sloops slope
and watch it sink
written in the blackest of inks
despair was tattooed on my skin
these the markings of your kin
a metaphor beyond your ken
an orphan's wings once clipped by cant's
now flying free on the winds of cans

Lets make amends, remove these burdens
from our backs then travel back to understand
you made a Son set at dawn on the peak of his own horizon
I've spent too many years compromising
I focus in on only all the positives felt
God bless the child that has its own
sense of self

Marcus C. John

<u>Blunt Speech</u>

It begins with a declaration
say "we the people" but maintain
the separation, state the rules
but don't amend them, prosecute the innocent,
promote straight and narrow in a crooked system
institute hypnotic tactics, always keep them distracted
cause dependence with devastation,
create the illusion that we need preparation
for invasions from nations we provoke
a masterful ruse, right before the eyes of the group
unamused, not everyone survives the punch of the joke
without the proper education, discombobulation
consumes and dooms the population
with false, phony, moral, mayoral inaugurations
leaders elected, to keep the masses recessive
compromised choices are only 3/5's accepted
white wash the benches and stain the prisons with colors
separate children from their fathers and brothers
Give claims of reparations, without respiration
supply welfare like air and teach them to inhale
while smoking is no longer allowed around here
But now I've seen it all
the European gaul
making green off the green
that keeps so many in cells
getting high off your own supply,
raising statuses off sales
earning profit off prophets so your legacy can last
all deliberately, oh lady liberty
why allow so many of your sons to only puff and not pass
thrown away like the leaf, clipping futures is the point
focused on the grass rooted, roll them all into the joint
The fear of losing freedom makes us scared to say it bluntly,
but America, you put the cunt in country

<u>Miseducation of the Brown</u>

Genocide! Genocide!
They're trying to masquerade a genocide!
Kill the people right before your eyes!

Building buildings by the waterside
Heard the story from water's side
I only hope one day the waters rise
and cleanse the Earth and make it purified
of all the lies that have been glorified

Our history stripped from the textbooks,
looted like our lineage
diluted depictions of our heritage, written by heretics,
permeating the minds of children, those blanks will be filled in

Remember Shaka, Remember Musa,
Remember Nefertiti, Remember Mwanga,
Remember Ramasses, Remember Imhotep,
Remember Kemet, Remember Nzingha,
Remember Osiris, Remember Isis,
Remember Ra, Remember Heru,
Remember Obatala, Remember Yemoja,
Remember Esu, Remember Osun

Being chained was never a choice
enslavement was not apart of our legacy,
it preempted it, like a virus to a cell
the introduction of a foreign species into a healthy
organism, caused disease, made us listless
but no matter how high the temp, we had some healers for the sickness

Remember Harriet, Remember Sojourner,
Remember Touissant, Remember Nat,
Remember Martin, Remember Malcolm,
Remember Marcus, Remember Claudette,
Remember Rustin, Remember Adam,
Remember Stokely, Remember Medgar,
Remember Huey, Remember Eldridge,
Remember Betty, Remember Coretta

Marcus C. John

So mad that Black don't crack they gave it to us,
in vain, not realizing our ascension was predestined,
first took rock and scribed tablets, made lyrics appear like magic
tapped in toe, scat in bebop, sung in sorrow, penned in poem,
rapped on fire, ancestral hymns deep within, all released with timing
melodies for the melanated dipped in platinum, gold, and diamond

Remember Langston, Remember Ella,
Remember Zora, Remember Duke,
Remember Miles, Remember Nina,
Remember Chuck, Remember Lou,
Remember Curtis. Remember Marvin,
Remember Michael, Remember Whitney,
Remember Left Eye, Remember Guru,
Remember Tupac, Remember Biggie

The revolution will not be televised, neither will the truth
this revolution is more like a cycle, watch the media spin
the proof; accentuate poverty, cause divisions within society
they create hysteria among those alike, while we fight our own reflections
and run for cover to those who assume the roles of false protection,
Your minds your greatest weapon

Remember Emmett, Remember Amadou,
Remember Abner, Remember Rodney,
Remember Eric, Remember Ferguson,
Remember Mike, Remember Ramarley,
Remember Officer Ridley, Remember Stephon,
Remember Eleanor, Remember Sean,
Remember Antwon, Remember Ms. Danner, Remember Sandra,
Remember Trayvon

Genocide! Genocide!
They're trying to masquerade a genocide!

Kill the people right before your eyes!
Kill the people right before your eyes!

<u>Punctuation</u>

Too many commas without periods,
my relationships have been a compilation
of run on sentences

Spent years tallying marks
in partnerships comparative to jail time
its like they ran on sentences

No escape. Stroked the keys
but couldn't find the
one to free myself

My type, indescribable
Uncommon to common literature.
Instead of a novel, I settle for
open letters with no bodies,
Sincerely yours becomes my signature.

The back space of my mind recalls
a simpler time when journaling was the norm
I miss those days in comparison
Now all avid note takers,
we find it easier to paraphrase
Ignoring our paragraph forms

Keeping tabs and saving files,
collecting all statistics
vacant verses without endings
finding comfort in ellipses

Social posts replace sonnets
the writers block cause solar eclipses.
A world wide web tacked to
a sky that is lacking illumination,
over lovers romanticizing like as light
puts the Sun in quotations

Marcus C. John

John 1

Fragment speech, curt language,
and open ended ideas;
My heart is an unedited dissertation,
Needing to be proofread

As I shift, enter, and return back to center,
I alt my perception and regain command,
control my functions, remain in stance,
more than in love, never falling, page up
ready for print. No more dear John letters
written in different dialects, I will stick to the script
Being the noun, adjective, and verb form of it...

stop

The Book of John

Part 2

<u>Open The Door</u>
Haiku #3

To all those trapped in a closet
but still feeling naked,
nude fits you

Marcus C. John

The Lover

It started off like any other morning
we were both wearing black
bodies still as cadavers,
your face read like an obituary
my eyes stared into the sarcophagus of our love;
even though it remained sleep, I was fully awake,
and this was a wake

The feeling of what it means to fail
reactions were off the richter scale
shaking, I pretended not to lose balance
even though the ground was quaking
you, sturdy as a doorframe safe from the collapse
we, both had different versions of support
I was yours, and so were you

In the beginning, you were smooth,
and clean, but underneath as weak as glass
perception blinded me to this reflection
of my past, mesmerized by the allure,
while the shine disguised the residue,
framed to be the perfect image,
funny how mirrors can play tricks on you

Shattered, I pieced together the parts of the road that brought us here
remembered I played passenger as you steered away from commitment
forgot my tainted heart was placed in park, but you were parallel,
then put it in gear. I take the blame for not buckling up,
we were destined for the crash, but the speed was addictive,
and I was afflicted to how you maneuvered the wheel

This lane of seduction turning into desire
only made both our flames burn higher
it was sweltering, the heat caused combustion
eruptions just from touches, clothes were torched to the seam
At our peak, bodies moved like the energy of steam
two freaks off the leash that could keep the momentum
crazy pillow talk between the sheets, it was bedlam

A roller coaster of emotions, rode every ride in the park
just for our amusement, but this trip had no theme
it was confusion, trance like in a state of free falling
with nothing to grasp, it was more like an illusion,
a fun house, reflective of our principles
but we saw this act before
its funny how mirrors can play tricks on you

The breakdown,
slowly leading to a break up
knowing I needed to break through, these mirrors
you, a shadow of who I want to share my light with
your ego, blocked the rays my heart was shining like
a cloud of shame; the strain on my love became too heavy
jealousy rained on our parade, tears fell like confetti

I had to remember myself complete, not broken
recall back to a time when I was the prize, not just a token
and sentiment wasn't seen as sacrifice and truth
didn't cause turmoil, my fire burned for you
fortunately, it was lighting the rest of this path,
a way out of the tall grass

Our love always had two sides
it reminded me of a forked tongue
rattled by our reality, my movements became constricted
present conditions squeezed the life out of me
courage slowly slithered up my spine as your disregard
was swallowing me whole, completely unhinged
I wrapped my mind around the thought of freedom
and shed your memory like skin

Marcus C. John

Teal Tercet

Bold as Black
Pure as White
Vocal as Teal

Was always told to be silent
even whispered when I wept
held in everything, including my breath

"Those words you speak are dirty"
emotions here are expletives
there was no distinguish between cussing and crying

Dying, voices suffocated by the darkness
truth bent like light to breakthrough
we began wearing the shadows for warmth

It was colder than blue
wish my pride was permanent
instead it fades with the day

Erase the way we've been taught to draw conclusions
sketch a template of my own
color life in a shade of yellow

In hopes to brighten up the neutral grays
what a privilege to be the prototype
they see our presentation as preliminary

Even though we've been stamped approved
there's still a wash of the ignorance
it's a filter that we can't remove

Tried to stay inside the margins
for a world that won't imagine
contained the fire, refrained from passion

Exempted from exhalation
as if every breath was charged
but not with currency, electricity

John 2

Had to remind myself I was eccentric,
not electric;
that the truth was not frightening

It was freeing
unyielding in sentiment
knowing your purpose is cemented

We've been constructed in creation
self portraits of the Creator
Did you forget you were a living image?

Be Art
Be Free
Be Bold as Black

Pure as White
and VOCAL as Teal.
asè

Marcus C. John

Mama's Boy
"(featuring excerpts from the Willie Lynch letter)"

This world,
Mothers and Sons
prefabricated as Men and Women
"Test her in every way"
Its like a whisper
she doesn't remember the indoctrination
he doesn't understand his place in this construct
pitted against one another in misconduct
all in front of the stares of the child

Wild the upbringing, voices like alarms ringing
destiny daring the Dad to depart
"for orderly futures, special and particular
attention must be paid to the female and
the youngest offspring"
Alone in the jungle, stronger than vine
searching for a way out like ivy,
survivors, we become apart of the plan

A formula, better than breast milk
I played the sucker
another Oedipus complex in noir
mother fucker
It's not our fault
All our Daddies first names are Willie
we were lynched with the umbilical cord
before we even breached the womb
"keep the body and take the mind"
mothers picking up roles they weren't meant to assume

Chess pieces in a game I was never asked to play
He becomes a permanent pawn, dependent on age
"she being frozen with a subconscious fear for his life,
will raise him to be mentally dependent and weak,
and physically strong"
Both unable to see the board we're all on

I Can See in Color

Clear teardrops from scarlet eyes
wash away my sunny pastures
I can see in color

Brown skin stands out in a world that operates in shades of grey
fraudulent tan skin people see red, when they see Black folk
getting green from white collared positions
in turn, they pull onyx pistols and metallic switchblades
to stuff us in auburn coffins
I can see in color

Crimson pavement sectioned off by yellow tape
speak louder than words ever could
navy skies seem to hover over sepia ghettos no matter the time of day
to them it is The Wire, technicolor entertainment streaming out of their
idiot box, but to me it is home, a monochromatic metropolis where
sunbeams don't reach and rainbows stop short

Mahogany boys grow up to be grown men with golden aspirations
who settle for bronze achievements because their futures are opaque
options consist of fighting a pale war, in forest fatigue, killing beige babies,
in search of a purple heart, or
standing on obsidian corners, selling white powder, chased down by
boys in blue, only to wind up in orange jumpsuits
I can see in color

Chocolate girls grow up to be emerald eyed women, with pink nails,
blond extensions, bright accessories, with Brazilian thoughts
wondering if anyone can see through their opal facades and ruby tempers,
to cure their pastel fantasies of one day waking up and being high yellow

High yellow politicians seem to be blind to the politics that plague their
melanin infused brothers, melanin infused brothers pretend to be deaf to
the cries of their mocha dipped soul sisters, mocha dipped soul sisters want
to play dumb to the white lies that are fed to their golden boys and
diamond girls in this copper tone society
but I can see in color

Marcus C. John

and the color of deception is a money green, while the color of wrath stays murder red, so the color of lust must be pussy pink, thus the color of ignorance is our reflection, and I could run through the spectrum for a moment of connection, but the answers lay beyond this poem, color, and projection

and I can see your charcoal soul
because your eyes are transparent
and its apparent, so I keep my Black head in pearl clouds
searching for a silver lining, praying that the color of hope keeps shining
because the color of truth, is blinding
I can see in color

SNAP

To the Beat y'all…

::Snap::
::Snap::
Retrain all the Black girls,
Retrain all the Black girls

::Snap::
::Snap:: (come on ya'll!)
Retrain all the Black girls,
Retrain all the Black girls

::Snap::
::Snap:: (what they wanna do?)
Retrain all the Black Girls!
Retrain all the Black Girls!
Retrain all the Black Girls!
Retrain all the Black…::snap::

Mattel created Barbie thinking, "I'll refine em all"
he said, remove the Foxy Browns and replace them with China Dolls

Dilute the daughters image of a self reflecting Queen
and tell them Living single is the newest flava on the scene

An independent woman is the recipe now
but raising kids alone wasn't in your destiny child

Little Missy's in the street, a short skirt and four inch heels,
but I write to turn these mini Nickis' back to Lauryn Hills.

::Snap::
::Snap::

Oh snap…

<u>Wakanda Haiku</u>
Haiku #4

Black Americans wearing
Kente cloth calling it cosplay?!?!
stay tuned.

Ballad Mongers

Someone stole your song and tried to sell it for profit
made off with your greatest hit to date
replaced your peace with rage and took your joy away
it's unsettling how the harmony can leave you so unsubtle,
befuddled, you roll through life like a tumbleweed
in search of an honest breeze to whisk you to safety
unable to trust the advances of oxygen
breathing becomes an obstacle
that old tune won't escape from your head
it keeps replaying
we keep repaving
the same avenues that led us here
one way alleys that resemble roads
I once thought I traveled the world and back
only to realize it was a cul de sac
forgave myself for getting distracted
I heard my song playing on the radio
we must remember to stop singing for everyone
all audiences are not meant to be entertained
allow the set to change, let the heart renew
heed the process
reclaim your prowess
switch the frequencies
You are a maestro,
A conductor,
be magnetic!
Attract what you need, release what you don't
and remember, we were sent here with more than one note.

Marcus C. John

The Acrobat

Cartwheel
we were going around in circles
couldn't figure out where to land
directions lost from the beginning
tried to find myself, but the room was spinning
moving forward wasn't part of the plan

Handstand
to say the least
I was head over heels
still not ready to go
convinced upside down was right side up;
I settled for my position, being inverted became a comfort
but gravity was such a gentleman

Somersault
we tried to roll on cold shoulders
but conversations turned to combat, it was some assault
tumbling in a toxic cycle; steady on repeat, our words went viral
I attempted to stop adding to the views of our suffering
but regret spun around like it was buffering

Backflip
forgot love and pain were not the same
mistook aggression for affection, again
The naive me, always wanting to be apart of a team
brought my jonesing to a gymnast, believed it when you told me
uneven bars were better than a balance beam
had to let go to truly receive

On my feet
executed the dismount,
properly this time
I will no longer repeat the same routine.

Perfect 10!

The Book of John

Part 3

\

<u>Release Me</u>
Haiku #5

Love, I assume
when you spoke, the levies broke; tears flooded the room,
dam…

Marcus C. John

The RelationShip

"…we met while we were drowning"

deep within a sea of obscurity
we treaded the waters in search of relief
belief tested in the face of adversity
nervously we plunged into a lovers state of lure
certainly we would make it to shore,
sure

pounding were the waves,
every crash rang like a symbol in my ear
you remaining calm became a symbol for the dive
demystified the darkness with the starlight in your eyes
clutched our breaths like treasure as the levels began to rise

blinded by the brine, liquid almost seemed reliable
something as vast as the Ocean started to
resemble home, how our minds became pliable
the beauty astounding, there was a certain comfort
that we found in drowning, it felt like flying,
but we weren't

commitment on the surface stuck out like a shark's fin,
we avoided the subject like Jaws, continued splashing in our current
getting further swept away by the currents, the rarest of occurrences
with a whirlpool of deterrence, both traveling from previous ports
when our ships met, relationships wrecked!

a total wipeout, an up-anchor of the courses we thought we knew
still we went full throttle, ignored the warnings on the radar,
uncorked the message in the bottle, trusting feelings over the
logistics, we abandoned vessels that could no longer harbor the
high tides of our hearts, we walked our planks in prayer,
may bravery be a backstroke on the face of a new frontier

learned buoyancy off the coast, became a lifeguard always on post
breaststroking toward our future we, in spite of all the mutiny

cleared the water trapped inside our lungs, wary another word would come
alas we knew our fates would end, unless we made it out this bend

traveled many moons, and endless days bereft with fear and hopeless nays
to reach a place we'd know as land, built strong like rock but soft as sand

a private island destination without cause or reservation
a solo journey made for two, the greatest chance I took was you

We met while we were drowning,
ironically at the same time we were dying of thirst
roots desperately needing to be watered
greenery seeking to be grown
two center chakras open, never again to be closed
once thought our paths crossing was one of despair
but this voyage was a reminder, that life with no you
would be like living without Air

Marcus C. John

<u>Sound Doctrine</u>

speak to me in a language that i can understand
release words that so often get caught on your pallet
taste the succulence of only saying what is felt,
only saying what is kind, make it sexy if you don't mind
take the time so it's empowering to both you and i

be true. understand that we all have opinions,
each of us grounded to a life of perspective
forever trying to branch from the root
we hope that our visions can peer past the perimeters
put in place by our experiences and experience anew
however, if i should lose focus or neglect my blind spot
speak to me in a language that i can understand

forgive. relate. inspire. be pleasant.
turn a hurricane into a draft
remember life is all about assembling and disassembling
we tend to forget the brevity that words can hold,
souls in bodies, equipped with the power to lift or
create the descent

a curse and a blessing bestowed,
lets never be bound by silence
and open our hearts to the expression of free love
may we only hear the best
may we only say whats true
hum harmonies over bass lines
perfectly pitched to the groove

my ears are in tune to your dialect,
dedicated to our dialogue
you're my favorite monologue,
just speak to me in a language that i can understand
and i will always be here to listen

Get Me Bodied

Thankful as grace
more valued than a piece of daily bread
almost forgot the heavy burdens I carried were outside, not in
what a gluttonous sin, swallowed every bit of self suppression,
wrapped myself in an individualized package
then stamped my worth on sale
body betrayal
too seasoned to be unaware of the consequences
needed to shake the bad habits I racked up
this bland existence was making me salty
stewing in my own spices, change seemed flavorful,
yet sharp as a clove; had a hankering for healing
on the tip of my tongue so close I could taste it
stayed too long in the oven roasting on
indecision when I knew I was done,
ready for the banquet, way beyond the buffet
kept the temperature on low but now it was time to soufflé
rising to the occasion, gathering every ingredient needed,
I prepped a plan to process and
began to whip up my greatest recipe yet
hats off to the chef, mincing through the kitchen,
mastering each mechanism, took knowledge and applied it
worked this body like an appliance, established discipline without defiance,
emptied every mental cabinet and re-shelved them with the organic
it was mind over everything, stretching it beyond its limits,
releasing the shame weighted onto me by condition
formed these muscles to raise awareness
and hope to lift my people with me, made the promise to never
return to that place where I could dishonor my temple
may time purify these lungs to breathe again
decrystalize these eyes to see again
may this journey lend encouragement
be received and fed as nourishment
seized the day, crossed the finish line on my own marathon
the road was long, still gave it all I had to give

Marcus C. John

Big Pun voice; "I just lost 100 pounds, I'm trying to live!"
Its so hard to stay focused
but in the end we reap the bonus
And life is sweet, as we return back to the seed
and sample what truly matters, your world on a silver platter,
bon appétit
I sit and dine, with my reflection
and see a sugar honey pie, baked
to perfection, all the years starving for affection
now feeding off my own confidence
sustained sustenance, took my body back
finally started seeing myself as a full meal,
and not just a midnight snack

Holy Crap!
Haiku #6

the greatest deception:
transcribing twelve chakras
as twelve disciples

Symbols

Projections of perjury stain the glass without leaving a mark
sit back and watch as life imitates art
A blending of monotone mindsets mimic Michelangelo
the ambiance echoes the last judgements of an evangelist

Rituals from the righteous leave the audience in awe
spellbound by wizards in robes who hold their reverie
treachery beneath the steeple, masquerades within cathedrals
bravos to the broken leading spiritual upheavals

Planetary alignments have open minds as well bibles
tribal, stars be my renaissance and religion
ancestors guide me as I formulate decisions
devils torment the heart as we approach ascension

Eye allowed me to see again
traveled mountain trails to find the peaks of yin
prayer protected me as I was weakening
but the strength that I was searching for I found it deep within

With no preparation for the toll
this was excavation of the soul
an uncovering of untold truths,
proof, revelations in pursuit

Perhaps the discovery was me in the manger,
me in the temple,
me on the cross
Remember what we have lost

Recollect the pieces
listen for my conscious and remind myself what peace is, and isn't
fractured servants with sermons of forms of control
how can one define holy, without being whole?

SpirituaList

Sow The Land.
Tend to the grounds with nurture.
Respect the boundaries like nature.
Place the stones around the garden.
Treat the soil with care.
Remember why you are here.

Cleanse The Water.
Make sure it stays purified.
Drink only when necessary.
Provide to those who come to you.
Try not to chase the thirsty.
Remember you are worthy.

Fan The Flame,
but don't mock it.
Use it for guidance,
For courage, and to inspire.
Shine your light.
Lead them out of the dark, but
Remember your heart.

Filter The Air.
Avoid the polluted.
Detoxify if needed.
Seep with pride, Be gusty.
Work well with others.
Don't forget about your sisters,
Remember your brothers.

Stay mindful, space exists inside us as well
spirit filled, made of stars, moon and planet
suns on earth
beings beyond
humans becoming
souls remembering and retaining,

These Gods are within

This isn't subtle
evolution never is
neither is love, neither is truth
but we stand in it all, living examples
of something more, something radical
something great, something magical,

Remember…

<u>Worry Free</u>

I've decided to live my life worry free
I've decided to live my life worry free
giving thanks for days I've been blessed to see
with the faith that this path was designed just for me

Starting with the breath,
each step, never taken for granted
head swirling in the clouds
but my feet stay planted
meditation was the key when enlightenment stopped
I had to master all my thoughts and psychological locks
then break free, stretch every inch of my human being
and remind myself that we were all God, as a humans being;
that forgiveness is essential and limits are mostly mental
and we manifest the things we put our energy into
I stay focused, knowing what they feed us is bogus
all their truths are GMO's, starving people stay hopeless
shoving lies down our throats, that only deprive us
with no nutrients or taste but these bars are high fiber
made from the best stuff on Earth
alchemy in every line plus alignment in verse
born with the understanding of controlling these chakras
remember not to let effects affect your tabula rasa

I've decided to live my life worry free
I've decided to live my life worry free
in my skin, everyday breathing comfortably
not defined by a check or a luxury

Forever rich in spirit
still mending debts that we inherit
life is always for the living but
some living lose their merit
they get caught up in the fantasy,
manipulate reality, covet words incessantly
forget about integrity, but we see this world as heavenly
a chance to heal the wounds, sustained on the journey here

Marcus C. John

and overtime pain can consume, so when they lack the will to care,
we will look out for the cure, and find it lurks within our core,
we just gotta play the chords,
that'll open up the passageways and neutralize the blockages,
Mind, Body, Spirit, an equation worth acknowledgement
a spell within the numbers, add them up, then read the caption
cause when I broke it down I started seeing words as fractions
simplifying problems, that equal action
moving forward without looking back
and

I've decided to live my life worry free
I've decided to live my life worry free
diving deep to depths of my destiny
shining light on the past momentarily

I hit the ground, face first, and lost all memory
searched for answers outside, but heard a voice telling me
Remember the process: ready, set go, relax, relate, release
then you must decide, is this completion or repeat?
A chosen co-creator reflecting divine light
connected by each breath, guided by my third eye sight
staying young at heart but relaying through the ages,
head for the ray as we fray through the mazes
one day they'll be singing our praises!

I've decided to live my life worry free
I've decided to live my life worry free
physically, mentally, and ethereally,
consciously, happily, and always me

<u>…In conclusion</u>

```
                                              F   L       N   G
                                        .           Y   I
s                                   .
t                               .
a                           g
n                       n
d                   i
i               u   p
n           j   m
g walking  r  u  n  n  i  n  g
```

<u>Crown Readjustment</u>
Haiku # 7
Oh right! Now I remember.
I only fell, because I was flying.

-Everything looks the same when you're up.
Now dust off, forgive yourself, and get back up,
up, and away!

Peace.

Marcus C. John is a Writer, Teacher, Poet, MC, and Brother to many. This book is an expression of growth and experience as the individual and a part of the group. High Power, Universal Consciousness, Honesty, and Love is what lives between these pages. Enjoy with an open mind and heart. Feel free to disengage if you need to. I hope this offering can inspire compassion, empathy, and communication to be back in front. Peace.

Made in the USA
Middletown, DE
18 March 2019